A PRAISE ANI
CHRIST

MW01599211

HIS KINGDOM SHALL NEVER END

CREATED BY KIM NOBLITT

ARRANGED AND ORCHESTRATED BY J. DANIEL SMITH
NARRATIONS WRITTEN BY LAWRENCE KIMBROUGH

PRODUCTS AVAILABLE:

Choral Book 0-6330-9264-9
Listening CD 0-6330-9256-8
Listening Cassette 0-6330-9246-0
Accompaniment CD (Split track) 0-6330-9247-9
Orchestration 0-6330-9257-6
Rehearsal Tracks 0-6330-9261-4
Posters (pack of 10) 0-6330-9249-5
Bulletins (pack of 100) 0-6330-9248-7
CD Promo Pak 0-6330-9289-4
Cassette Promo Pak 0-6330-9269-X

GENEVOX

INSTRUMENTATION

**His Kingdom Shall Never End • Thou Didst Leave Thy Throne •
We Crown You Lord of All • His Kingdom Shall Never End (Finale)**

Flute 1-2, Oboe, Opt. Soprano Sax (for Oboe), Clarinet 1-2, Trumpet 1, Trumpet 2-3,
F Horn 1-2, Opt. Alto Sax (for F Horn), Trombone 1-2, Opt. Tenor Sax (for Trombone 1-2),
Trombone 3/Tuba, Rhythm, Harp, Violin 1, Violin 2, Viola, Opt. Clarinet 3 (for Viola),
Cello (Bassoon), Opt. Bass Clarinet (for Cello), String Bass

Holy One • I Have Found the King • Come Light Your World

Trumpet 1, Trumpet 2-3, Alto Sax, Tenor Sax, Opt. Trombone (for Tenor Sax),
Trombone 1-2, Opt. Baritone Sax (for Trombone), Rhythm, Violin 1, Violin 2, Viola,
Opt. Clarinet (for Viola), Cello (Bassoon), Opt. Bass Clarinet (for Cello), String Bass

Magnificat • Look at My Son

Flute 1-2, Oboe, Opt. Soprano Sax (for Oboe), Clarinet 1-2, Rhythm, Harp, Violin 1, Violin 2,
Viola, Opt. Clarinet 3 (for Viola), Cello (Bassoon), Opt. Bass Clarinet (for Cello), String Bass

My God, My King

Soprano Sax, Rhythm

**Forever Is Here • Not So Silent Night • Firstborn •
God with Us • Waiting • Willing
(All Narrations)**

Rhythm

During the process of recording this work for the demonstration recording,
many percussion instruments were improvised by session players. These parts have not
been written out in either the score or in separate parts. Percussionists preparing this
music for worship use are advised to listen to the demonstration recording to develop
ideas for creating their own improvised parts.

The rhythm part in this orchestration is designed to provide satisfying accompaniment
throughout. However, keyboard players may find it helpful to reference certain passages
in the choral score to supply the most supportive accompaniment.

FOREWORDS

I am delighted to share this new Christmas work, *His Kingdom Shall Never End*. The prophet Isaiah said it best:

"For unto us a Child is born,
Unto us a Son is given;
And the government will be upon His shoulder.
And His name will be called
Wonderful, Counselor, Mighty God,
Everlasting Father, Prince of Peace.
Of the increase of His government and peace
There will be no end,
Upon the throne of David and over His kingdom,
To order it and establish it with judgment and justice
From that time forward, even forever.
The zeal of the Lord of hosts will perform this." [1]

Isaiah 9:6-7

The birth of Jesus ushered in "a whole new life—a whole new tomorrow—a whole new forever—that nothing and no one can take away from us." As believers, we are experiencing the effects of His kingdom, which is still working 2000 years later and "shall never, ever end."

His Kingdom Shall Never End takes a fresh look at the biblical narrative found in the Gospels of Matthew, Luke, John, and the Book of Isaiah. Three worship leaders (two men and one woman) narrate and sing most of the solos; however, you are not locked into that. It is a very flexible work, so let your creative imaginations run wild. It was recorded with a smaller group to show its flexibility.

My new friend, Lawrence Kimbrough, wrote brilliant narrations. He did a masterful job of connecting the songs with the narrations, so they flow wonderfully together.

The songs are easily learned, and we have heard the cries of those who love lush, four-part choral pieces. J. Daniel Smith did a wonderful job with "Thou Didst Leave Thy Throne," "We Crown You Lord of All," and other songs. You will love these wonderful orchestrations.

I love the rhythm section, so there are some wonderful moments, such as the song "Holy One," co-written with Jamie Harvill. Consider using this song with your congregation during the Christmas season.

My desire is to help you plan for Sundays and special events by providing songs that can be used in multiple ways. Songs like "Magnificat" and the duet "Look at My Son" can be used in your Christmas pageant. The songs in this work may also be used as Sunday morning anthems with your choir and orchestra during the Christmas season, or the entire work may be used as a special presentation.

Kim Noblitt

Kim Noblitt

Let's face it, we live in a new day. Everything around us is in a state of change—methods are changing, music styles are evolving, and fresh faces are emerging in our choirs and praise teams. One thing that does *not* change is the Word of God and the truth it holds. The story of the birth of Christ will always be the same. Our challenge is to find creative ways to communicate that story. I think you'll find *His Kingdom Shall Never End* is a fresh approach to an old story. The sounds are more contemporary, but they do not sacrifice the traditional melodies we've grown to love. Kim Noblitt and his writers have crafted singable, exciting melodies and lyrics that are a joy to sing and that reflect the spirit of the season. Your choir will be refreshed with this worship opportunity. I pray the Light of the world will illuminate your season as you communicate this timeless message to your world.

J. Daniel Smith
Producer/Arranger

SEQUENCE

His Kingdom Shall Never End

with

Angels, from the Realms of Glory

Words and Music by KIM NOBLITT
Arranged by J. Daniel Smith

55

†Come and wor-ship, come and wor-ship,_____

Optional TENORS only

| Am7 | | D | D/C | | B | B7/D♯ | | Em | | E | D/F♯ | E/G♯ |

58 div. *ff* unis.

Wor - ship Christ, the new - born King!_____ His

div. *ff* unis.

| Am | G/B | Am/C | Em/C♯ | | G/D | D | E | | | D/E |

ff

61 div.

king - dom shall nev - er, ev - er end.____ Though

div.

| A | | E/A | | D/A | | A |

---

† "Angels, from the Realms of Glory." Words James Montgomery. Music Henry T. Smart.

Forever Is Here
Narration

Music by KIM NOBLITT
Arranged by J. Daniel Smith

*NARRATOR 1: No, His kingdom shall never, never, never end. The King has come!
He has roared down from the heights of heaven—like a Lion of Judah bounding
into our needy lives. When all was lost, when all we had to hope for was something
to get us through another day, Christ came, bringing us a whole new life—a whole
new tomorrow—a whole new forever—that nothing and no one can take away from us.

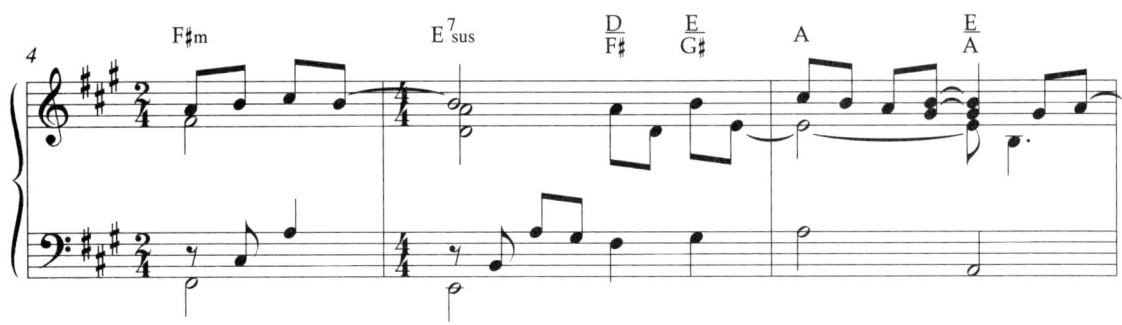

*NARRATOR 2: Jesus is here! Our King is here! Feel His touch on your heart.
Sense His presence deep in your spirit.

*NARRATOR 3: Come, let us take our rightful places around the throne of our
King...and worship Him!

Holy One

with

Angels We Have Heard on High

Words and Music by
JAMIE HARVILL and KIM NOBLITT
Arranged by J. Daniel Smith

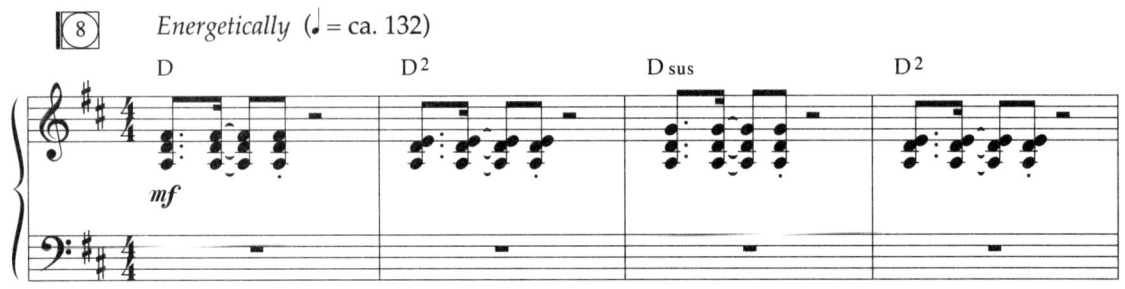

11

- est,_____ Je - sus, our Mes - si -

A sus   A   A² A   D   D²   D sus   D

15

- ah,_____ heav - en's per - fect Son.__

A sus   A   A² A   Em⁷

18

div.

You are the   long a - wait - ed One,___ we give__ You praise.__

div.

$\frac{D^2}{F\sharp}$ G² $\frac{G^2}{A}$

24

† "Angels We Have Heard on High." Traditional French Carol.

Magnificat

with

Silent Night

Solo and Ladies' Choir

Words and Music by KIM NOBLITT
Arranged by J. Daniel Smith

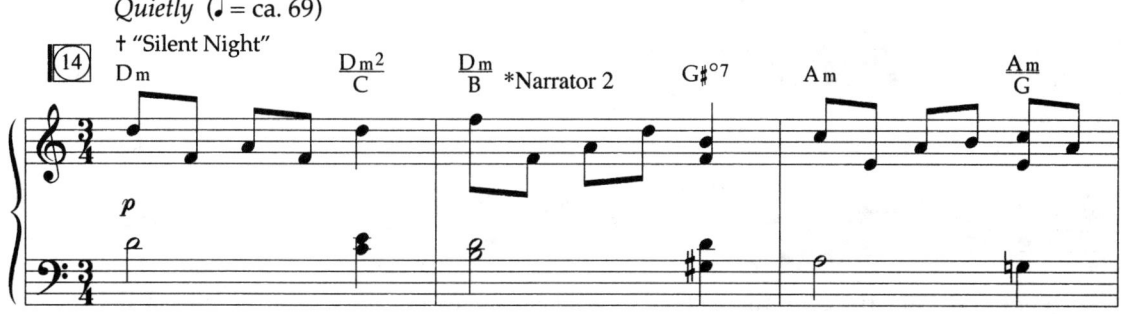

*NARRATOR 2: An angel appeared, and Mary's eyes grew wide with surprise. The angel spoke, and Mary's face grew pale in disbelief. The angel left, and Mary did what? She passionately gave praise to the Lord.

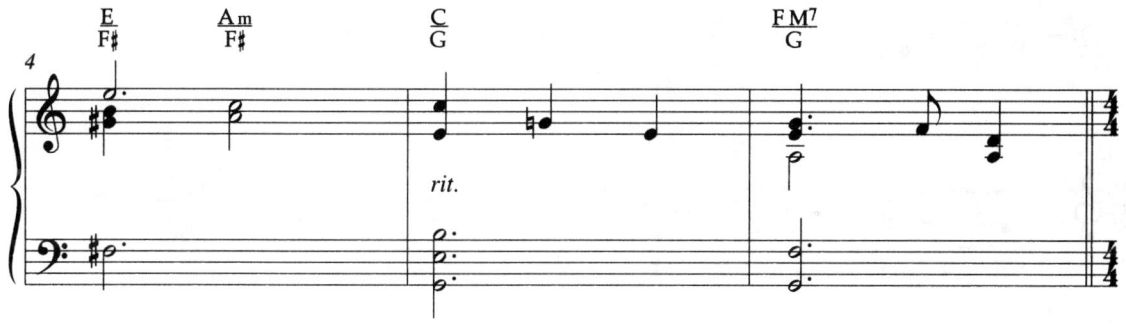

† "Silent Night." Music Franz Gruber.

SOLO (Mary) *mp*

My soul mag-ni-fies— You, Lord, glo-ri-fies— You, Lord, and re-joic-es in— You, my God and Sav- ior. My soul mag-ni-fies— You, Lord, glo-ri-fies— You, Lord, and re-joic-es in— You, my God and

36

Not So Silent Night
Narration

Music by KIM NOBLITT
Arranged by J. Daniel Smith

NARRATOR 3: *(without music)* The story seems so simple to us now. *(music begins)* I mean, don't we all have our little Marys and Josephs scattered around the house this time of year—little angels, little shepherds, little wise men? It's like we sometimes only see Christmas in miniature...in ways we can pick up in our hands and arrange around our lives.

*NARRATOR 1: But compare that smallness to how the shepherds must have felt, just standing around that night, expecting nothing out of the ordinary—when all of a sudden—boom!—it was Christmas!—the lights, the sounds! I'm telling you, if they were here today, well, I don't think the excitement would have worn off yet—not even after two thousand years!

*NARRATOR 3: And that's why we need to be here tonight…together…again…so that we can gather with others who share this mystery…so that we can again feel the heartbeat of the shepherds as they raced into town…so that we can skid into the doorway of a stable in Bethlehem…and stop…and kneel… *(continuing)*

(Segue to "My God, My King")

My God, My King

with

Away in a Manger

Words and Music by
ED KERR and KIM NOBLITT
Arranged by J. Daniel Smith

NARRATOR 3: *(music begins)*...and look into the face of our Savior and King.

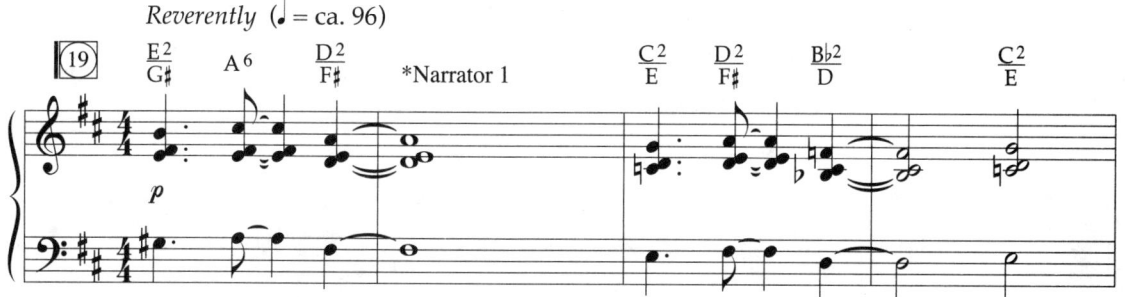

*NARRATOR 1: That's why we're here tonight, Lord. We want to see You again—not in little, predictable ways we've pictured You in our Christmas decorations, but in the eternal, life-sized fullness of Your being. O God our King, O Christ our Lord and Savior, we're here at Your feet. Please, show us Your glory.

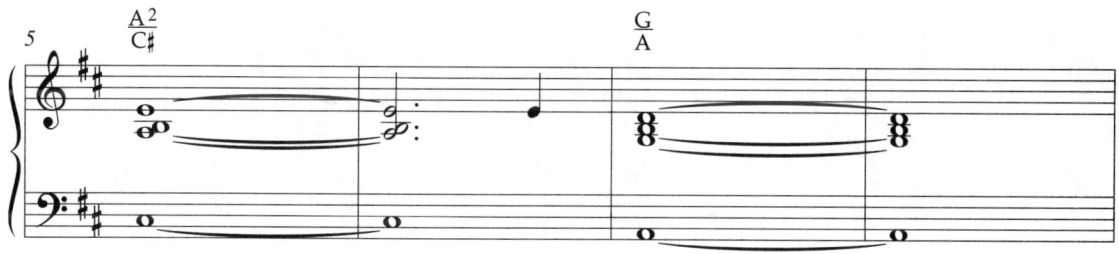

† "Away in a Manger." Words Anonymous. Music James R. Murray.

- ture sing.__ Christ the Lord__ is come__ to dwell, my God,__ my King.__ Hal-le-lu-jah,__ long a-wait-ed One.__ Hal-le-

My Lord,— my God,— my King.

p fading out

Firstborn

Narration

Music by
ED KERR and KIM NOBLITT
Arranged by J. Daniel Smith

Quietly (♩ = ca. 100)

†"My God, My King"

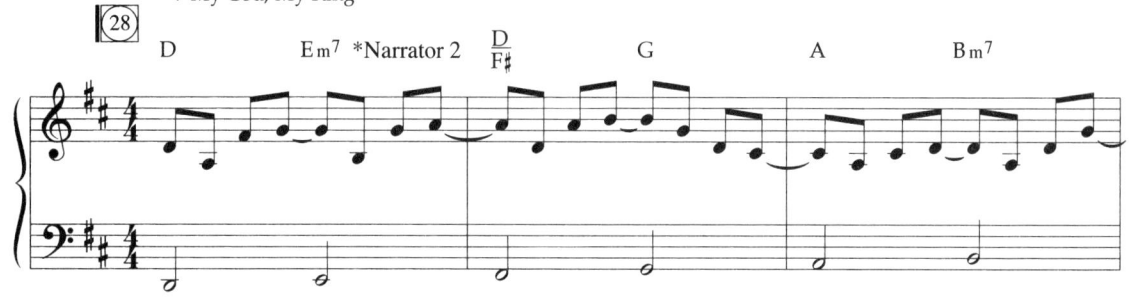

*NARRATOR 2: And though He was a King, He was still Mary's little Boy. No matter how unique the circumstances, He was still Joseph's newborn Son. Remember how that felt—to be first-time parents? I mean, they knew He belonged to God, but for right now…there He was, resting in their arms, curling His tiny hand around their fingers, looking up at Daddy with those big, innocent eyes.

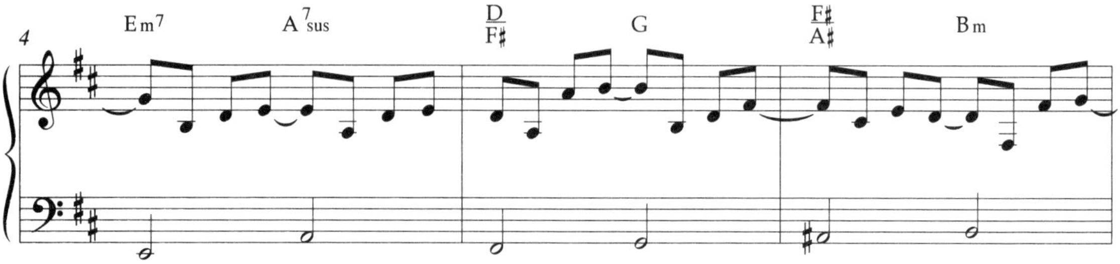

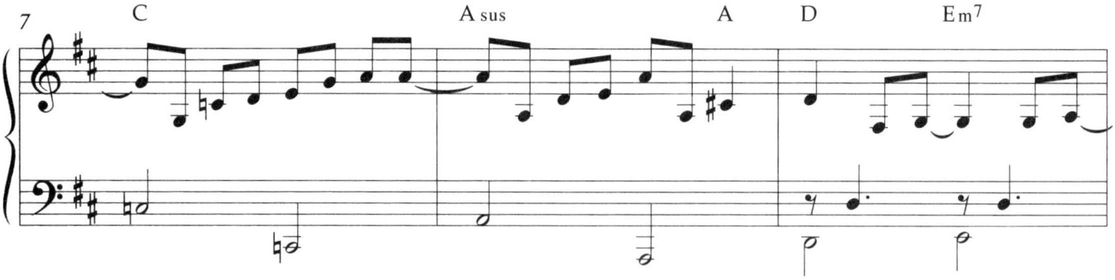

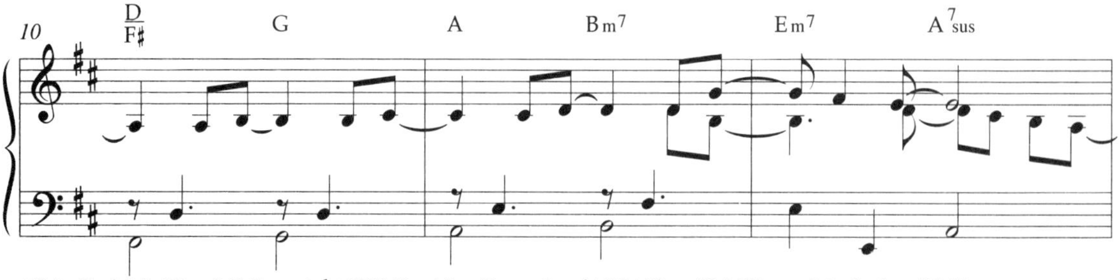

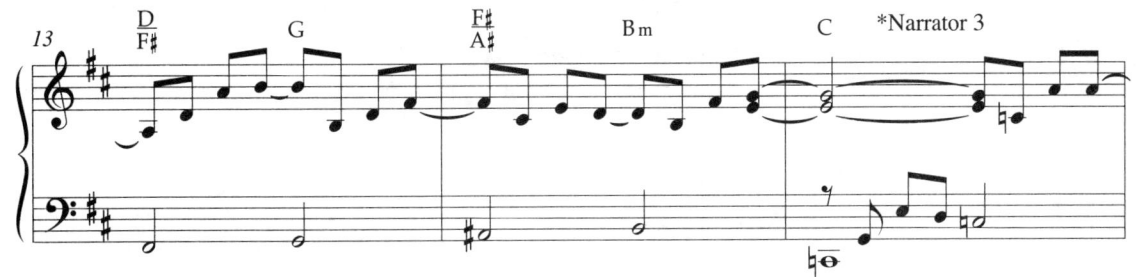

*NARRATOR 3: The Savior of the world…belonged to them!—to be raised in their home, to be part of their family. I'm sure that before He was born, they had prepared themselves to hold Him a little loosely (and God certainly must have known this), but how do you keep from wanting to show that little Baby to everyone who comes by: Do you know who this is? This is my Son. Isn't He something? This is my Son.

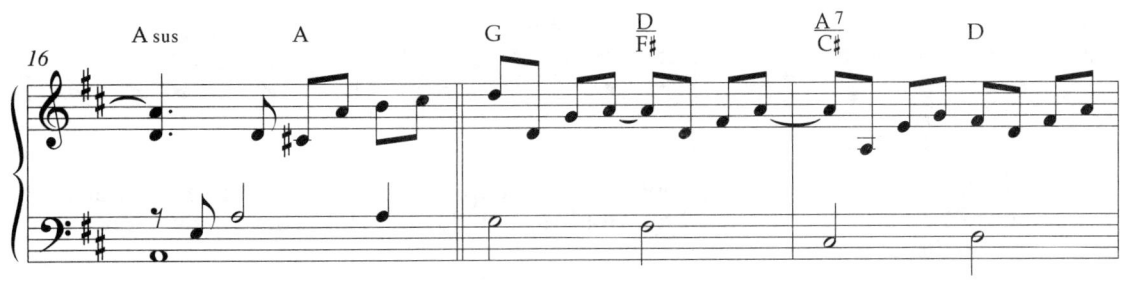

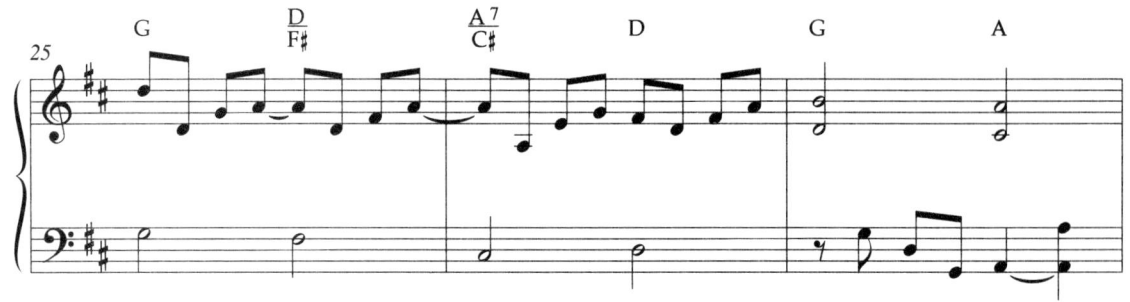

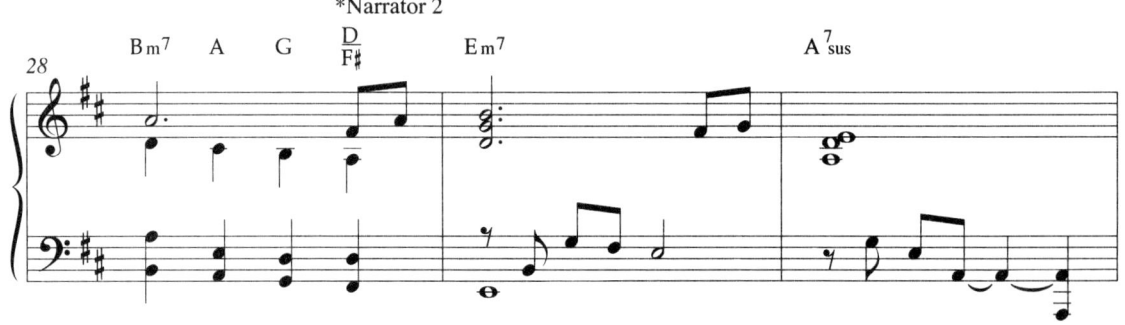

*NARRATOR 2: Hold Him up, Joseph. Hold Him up. He's the King we've been waiting for. He's the hope we've longed for. Hold Him up, Joseph. Hold Him up. Everyone, let's hold Him up!

Look at My Son
Duet and Choir

Words and Music by KIM NOBLITT
Arranged by J. Daniel Smith

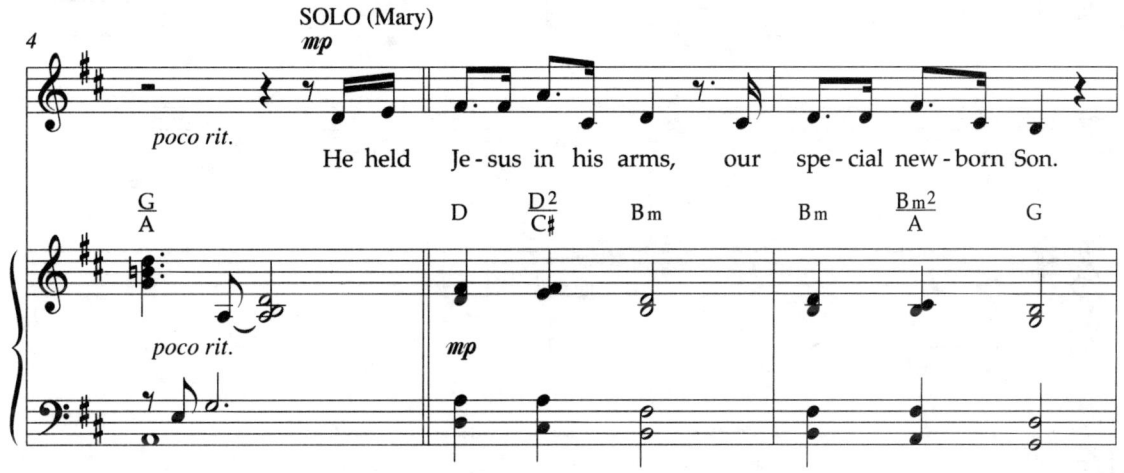

SOLO (Mary)

He held Je-sus in his arms, our spe-cial new-born Son.

Jo-seph___ held Him tight to keep Him warm. And the

be the Prom - ised One,— my lit - tle help - less Son?—

How could one— so small— change all the world? Why would

God's Mes-si - ah be— born in - to these hum - ble means?— Yet

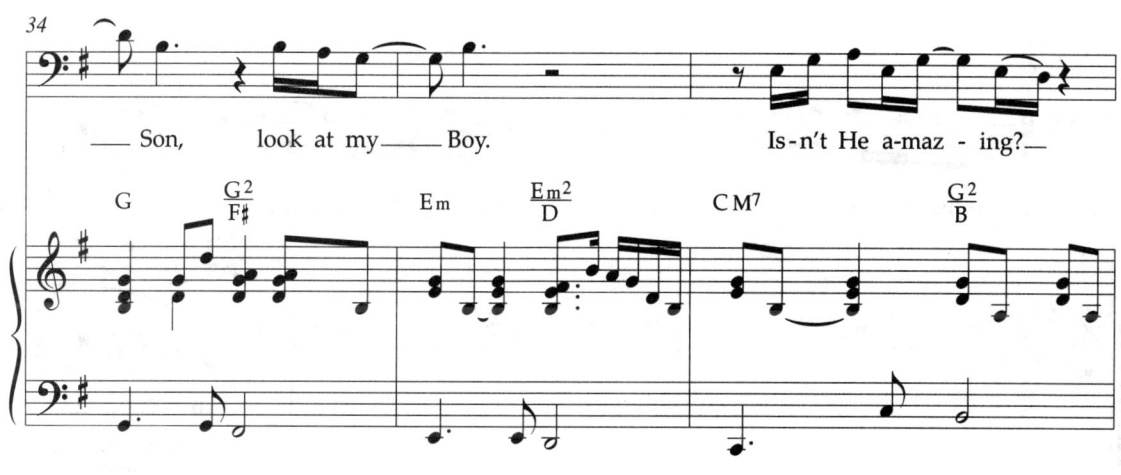

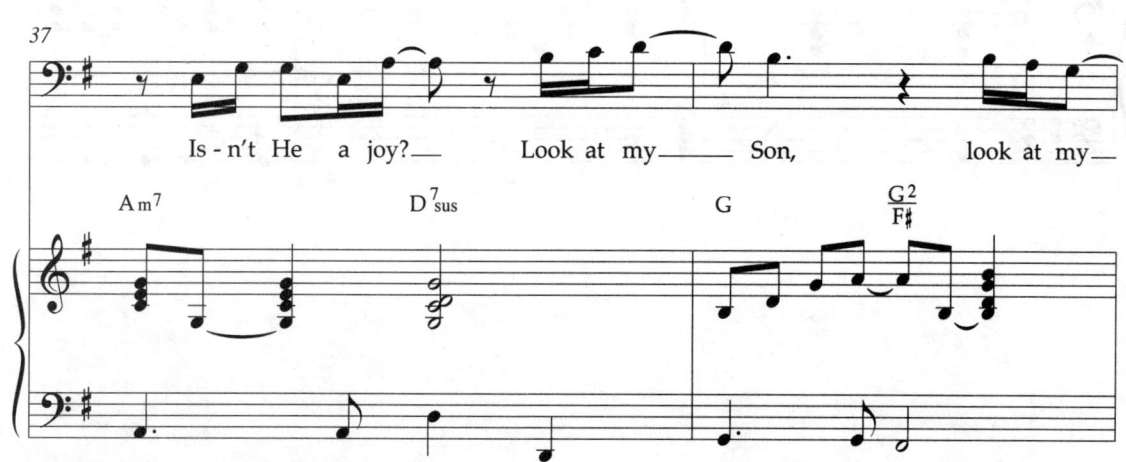

39

Em   Em²/D   CM⁷   G²/B

___ Boy.   Sal - va - tion for all has come,___   gath - er

33

41

'round me, ev - 'ry-one,___   and look at my ___ Son.___

CHOIR unis.
mp

Ah ___
mp

Am⁷   Am⁷/D   G

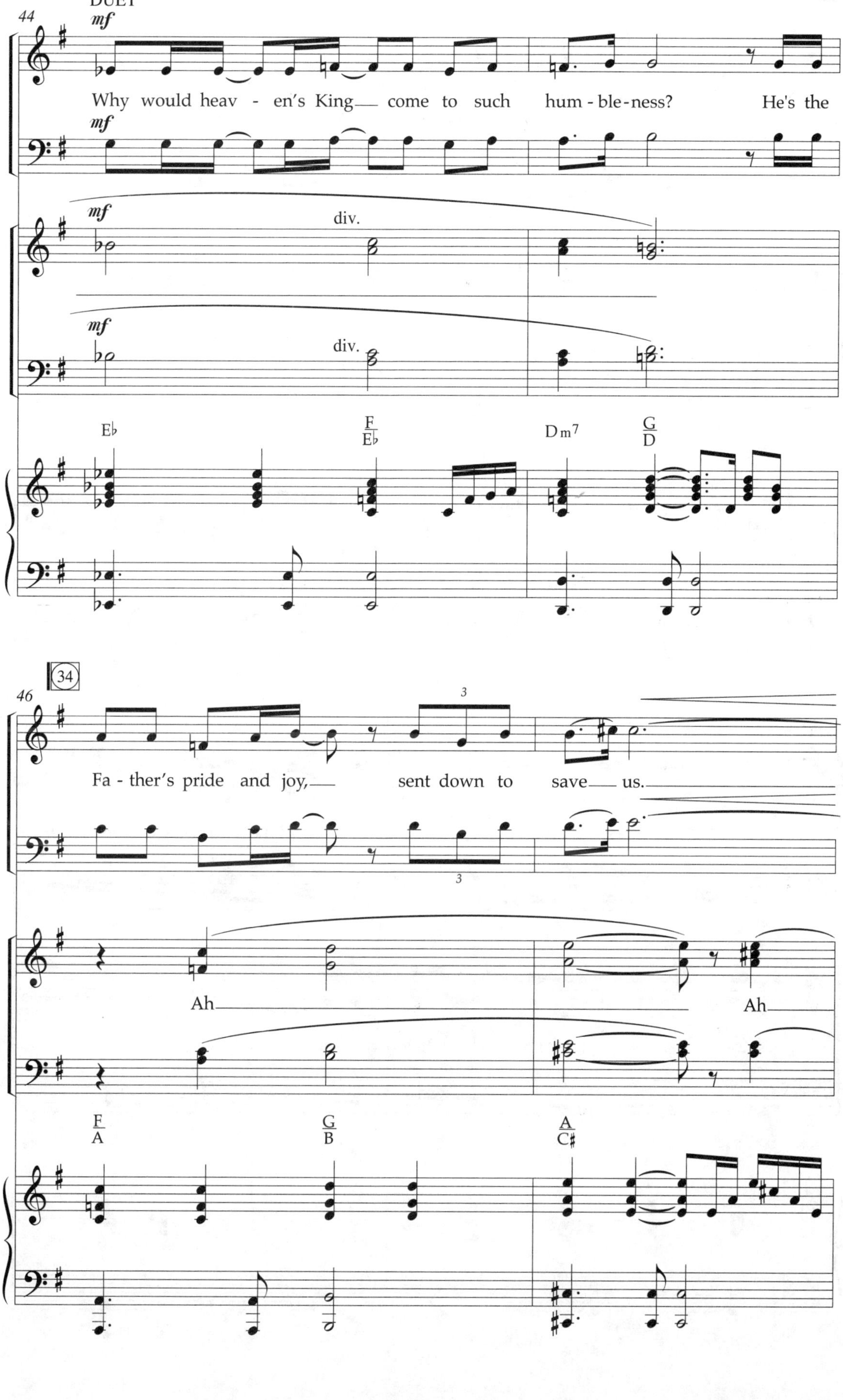
DUET
44
mf
Why would heav - en's King come to such hum - ble - ness? He's the
mf
mf
div.
mf
div.
E♭
F
E♭
Dm7
G
D
34
46
3
Fa - ther's pride and joy, sent down to save us.
3
Ah
Ah
F
A
G
B
A
C♯

God with Us
Narration

Music by KIM NOBLITT
Arranged by J. Daniel Smith

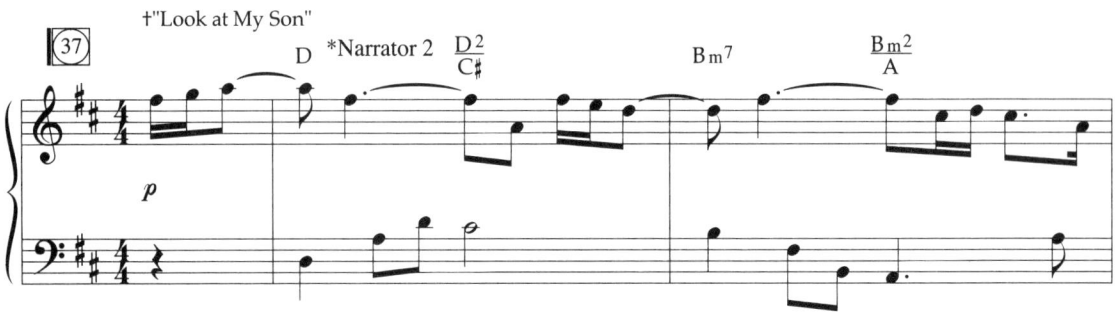

*NARRATOR 2: Lord, we want to hold You like Joseph held You—proudly and tenderly. We want to take You around to others so they can see for themselves that the King of glory has come to us with soft skin, a loving smile, and a human touch—that salvation has come and found us, that salvation has come to us in flesh and bone…and You're so near that they can reach out and touch You. *(pause)* Lord, when we look in Your eyes, we see a miracle. When others look in our eyes, Lord, may they see You.

I Have Found the King

with

O Come, All Ye Faithful
Trio

Words and Music by
ED KERR and KIM NOBLITT
Arranged by J. Daniel Smith

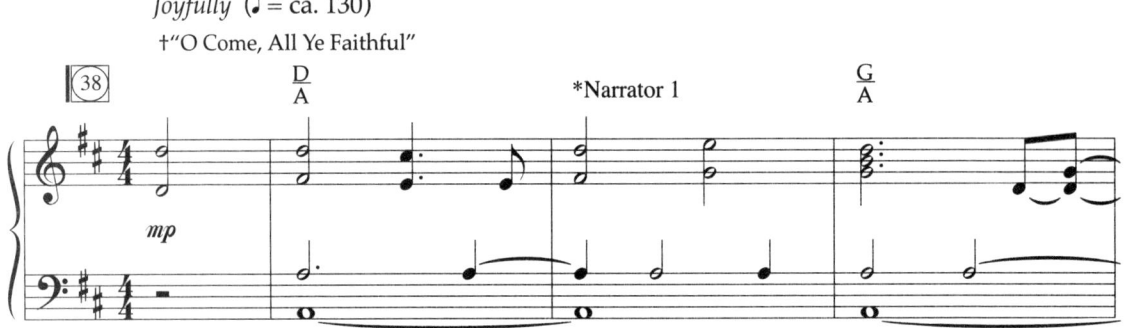

*NARRATOR 1: Yes, Lord, may they see You. Even if they start out a world away. Even if they're blinded by human wisdom. Even if they're not used to bowing to anyone. Make Yourself so clear, make Your glory shine so bright, that they see Your star in the sky…and they follow it to the end of themselves.

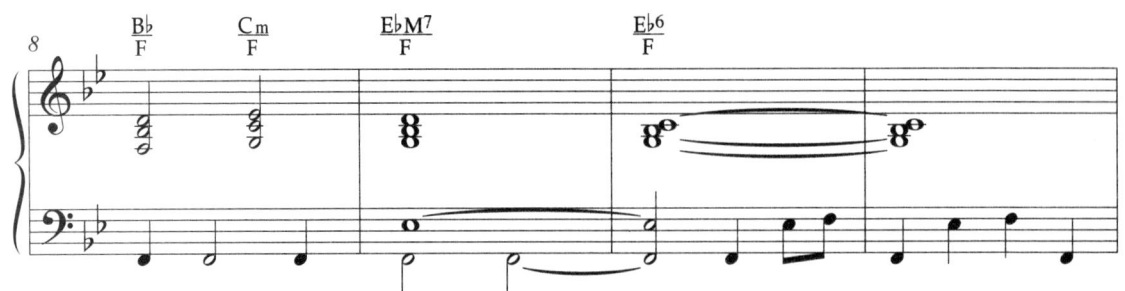

† "O Come, All Ye Faithful." Words Latin Hymn, ascribed to John Francis Wade. Music John Francis Wade.

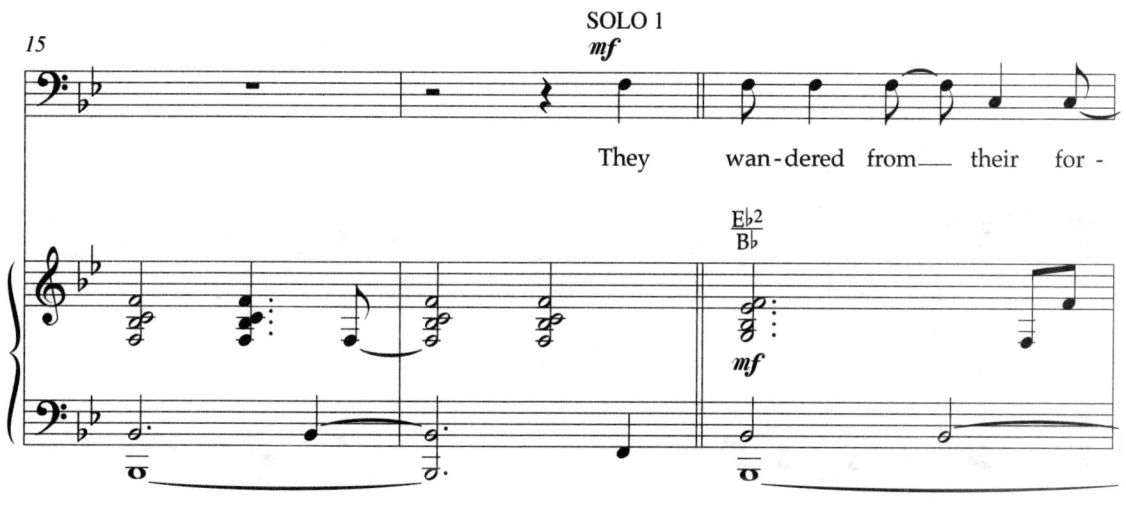

They wan-dered from— their for-

- eign land, bring-ing gold, myrrh,— and frank - in - cense. A

star was placed— up in— the sky   to lead them to— the One—

SOLO 2

— called Christ.— And so they crossed— the des - ert sand to the

lit - tle town— of Beth - le - hem. And when they found— Him, Christ—

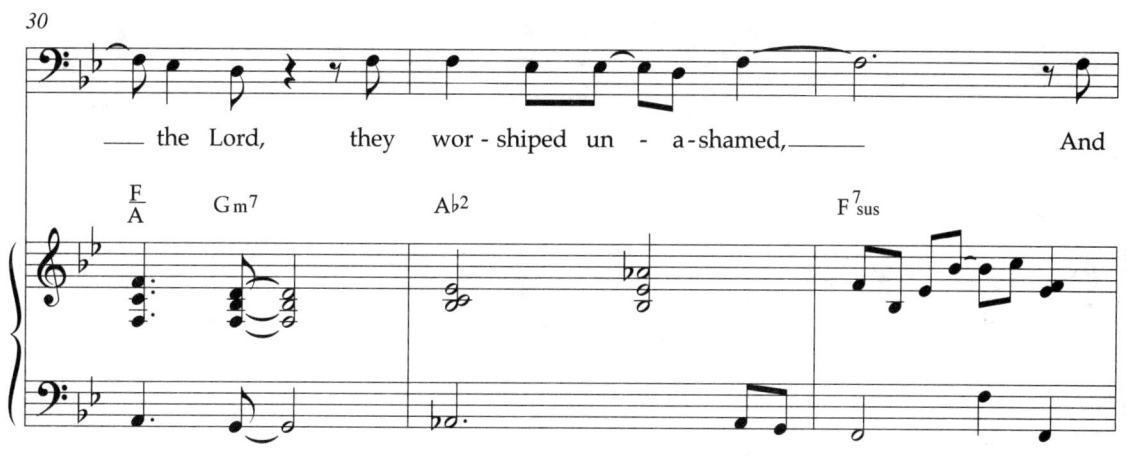

30

— the Lord, they wor-shiped un - a-shamed,___ And

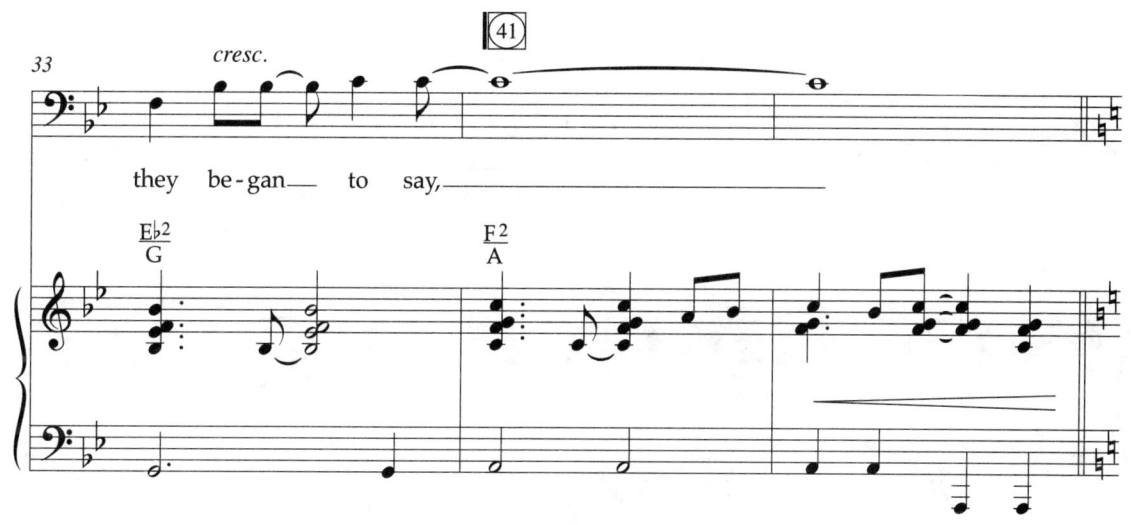

33

cresc.

they be-gan___ to say,___

TRIO

36 div.

"I have found___ Him, I___ have found___ the Sav - ior.___

I will bow—— down, bow——— be - fore—— the King.——

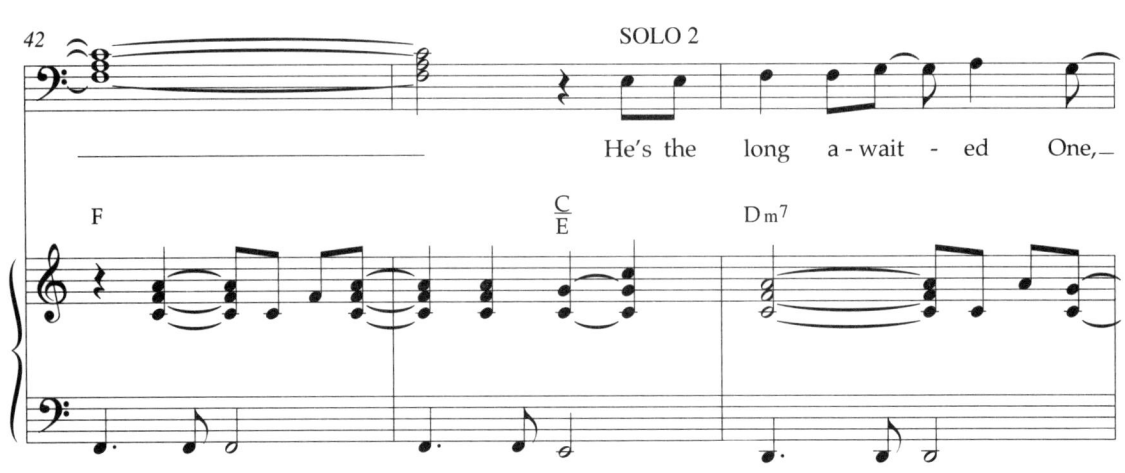

SOLO 2

He's the long a - wait - ed One,——

SOLO 3

45 2nd time

2nd time to Coda

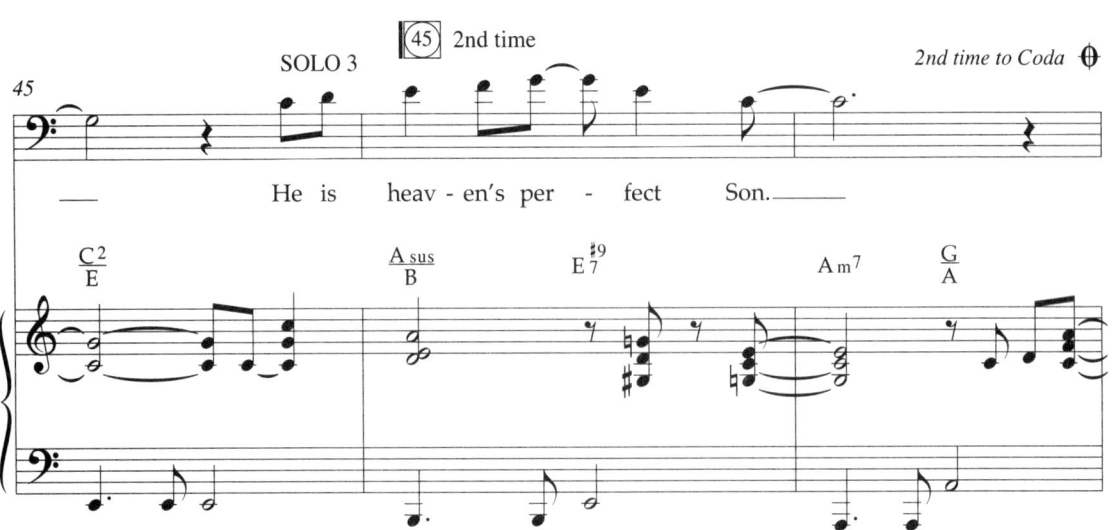

He is heav - en's per - fect Son.———

TRIO
unis.   div.

I have found— Him, I— have found— the King."

SOLO 3
mf

We don't need the star— of Beth-

-le-hem, nor the gold and myrrh or frank-in-cense. The

Ho-ly Spir-it is our Guide to lead us to the One

called Christ. The gifts we bring are ones of praise, Je-sus,

66

thank You for__ a - maz - ing grace.__ We wor-ship You,__ O Christ__

$\frac{E\flat2}{B\flat}$ $\frac{F}{B\flat}$ $B\flat$ $E\flat2$ $\frac{B\flat2}{D}$

69

__ the Lord,__ You came to seek__ and save.__ With

$\frac{F}{A}$ Gm^7 $A\flat2$ F^7_{sus}

cresc.   (44)   D.S. al Coda

72

hum - ble hearts__ we say,__

$\frac{E\flat2}{G}$ $\frac{F2}{A}$

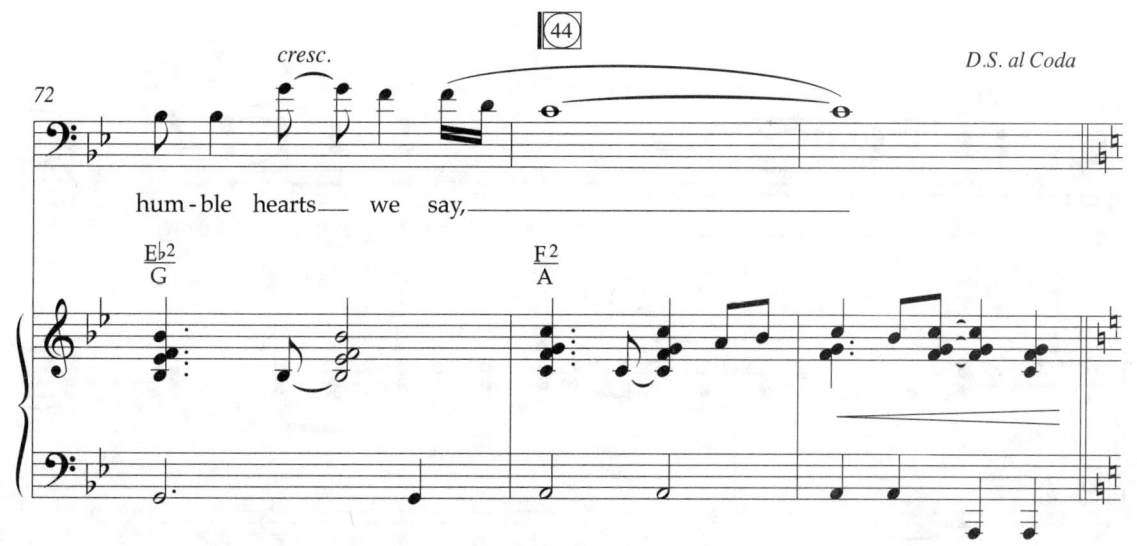

CODA

be - fore the King. He's the

long a-wait-ed One, He is heav-en's per - fect Son.

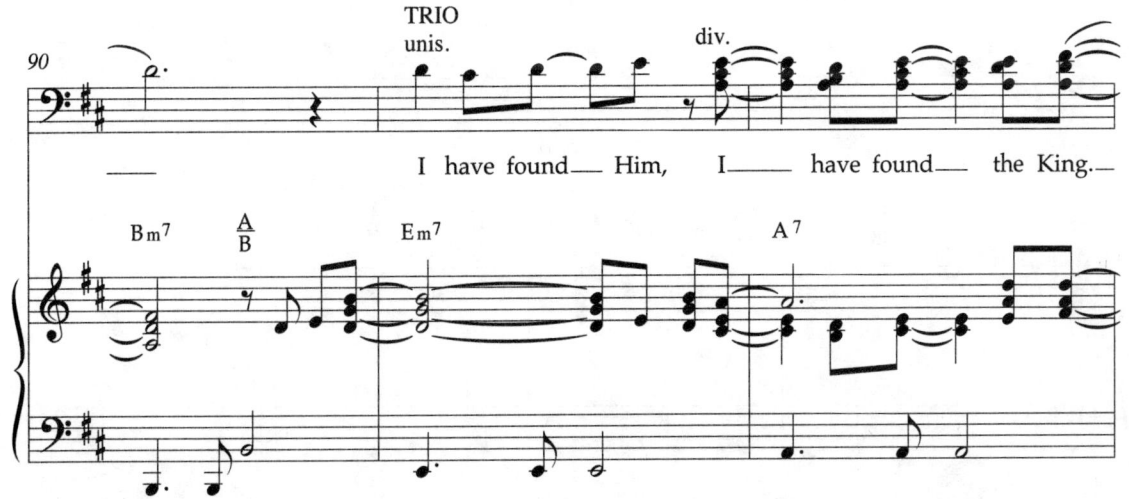

I have found Him, I have found the King.

I have found— Him, I—

—have found— the King." O

come, let us a - dore Him;—

Waiting
Narration

Music by ED KERR and KIM NOBLITT
Arranged by J. Daniel Smith

*NARRATOR 3: From being lost, to being found. From being without hope, to being without a doubt. From being surrounded and suffocated by the darkness, to being restored—reborn by the light.

*NARRATOR 1: Like old Simeon, tottering around the temple, waiting for years on a promise, waiting for the dark days of his people to come to an end, some of us sit here tonight…waiting. Waiting while our dreams grow dark. Waiting while our prayers grow cold. Waiting for Him to come, waiting for the night to lift.

*NARRATOR 3: He will come! I assure you, He will come. When the darkness has
   done all that God intended it to do, Christ will come, bringing hope. He will come,
   bearing His promise. Lord Jesus, come, come light Your world!

Come Light Your World

Soloists and Choir

Words and Music by KIM NOBLITT
Arranged by J. Daniel Smith

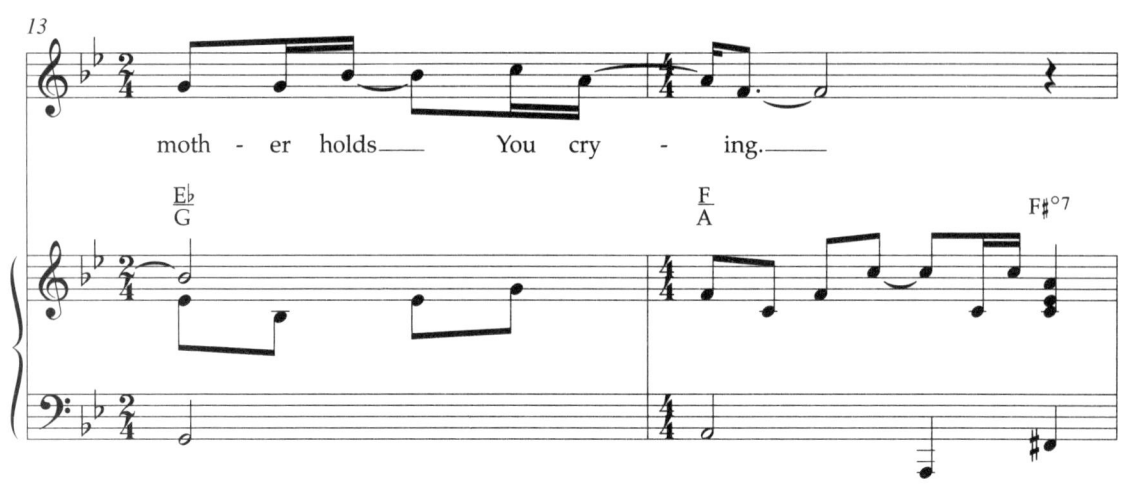

moth - er holds___ You cry - ing.___

Light of the world,___ I guess we just don't un - der - stand.___

Lord, we've been so long___ in dark - ness, will You

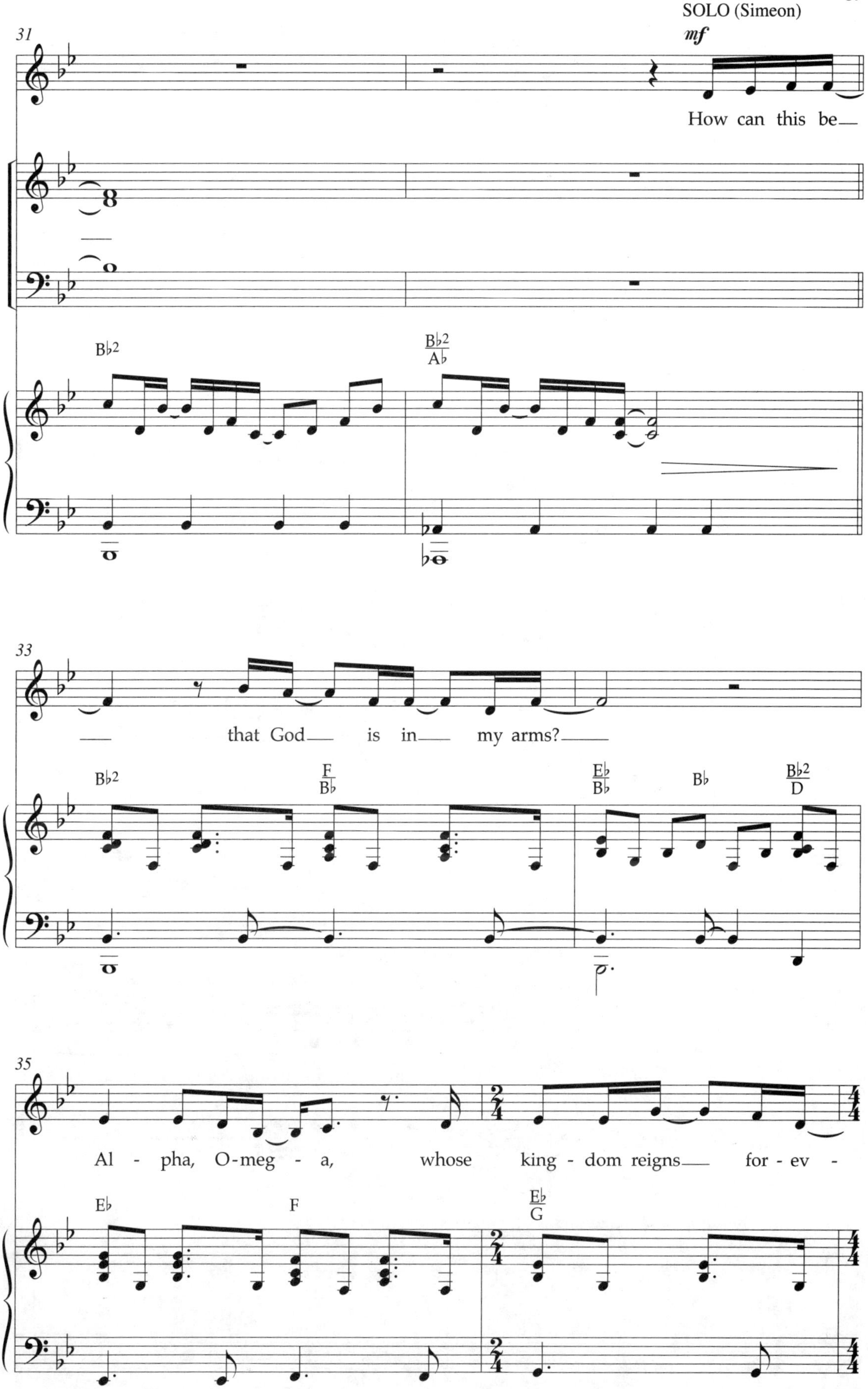
SOLO (Simeon)
mf
31
How can this be
B♭2
B♭2/A♭
33
that God is in my arms?
B♭2
F/B♭
E♭/B♭
B♭
B♭2/D
35
Al - pha, O-meg - a, whose king - dom reigns for - ev -
E♭
F
E♭/G

just don't un - der - stand._____ Lord, we've

unis.
just don't un - der - stand._____

unis.

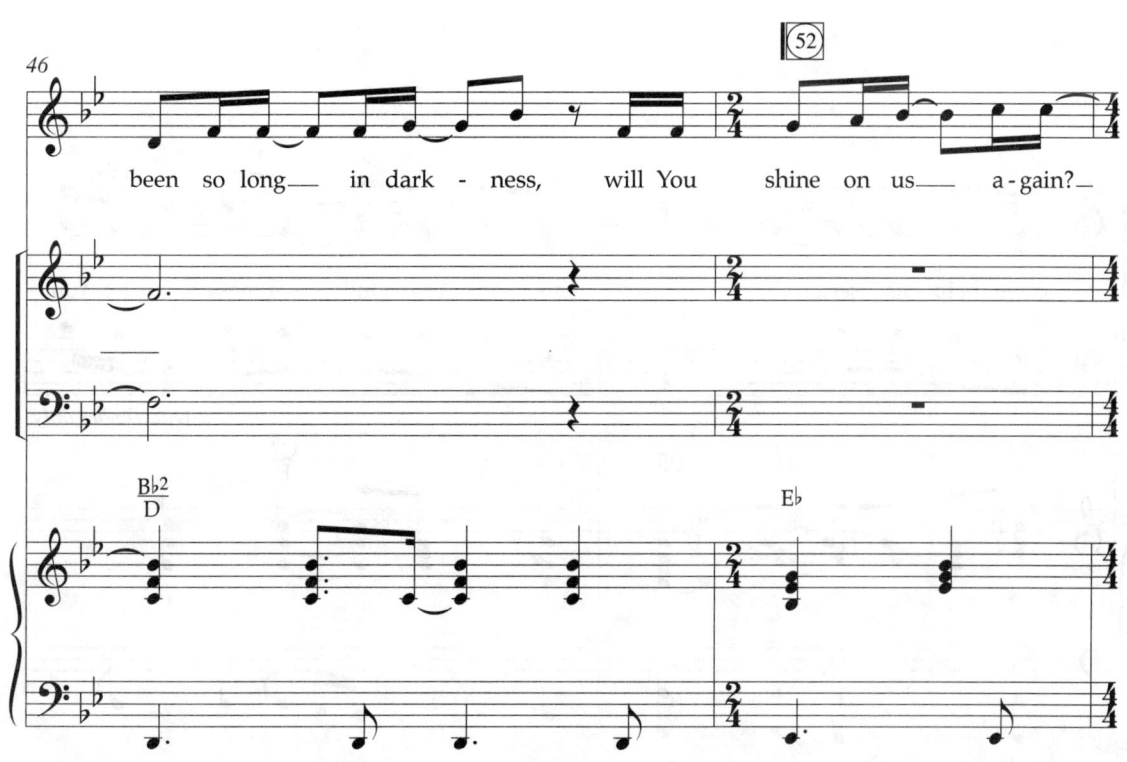

been so long__ in dark - ness, will You shine on us__ a - gain?__

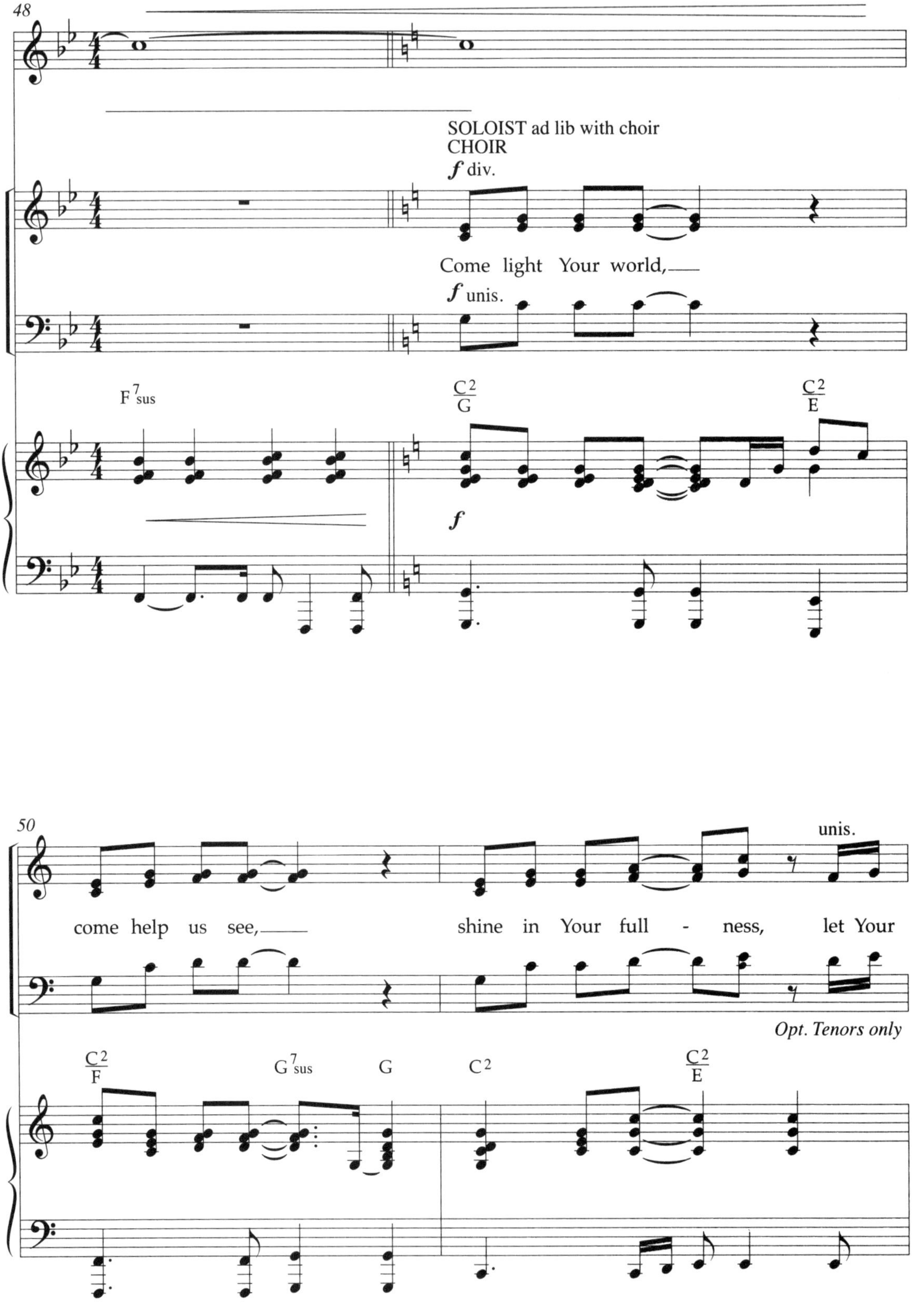
48
SOLOIST ad lib with choir
CHOIR
f div.
Come light Your world,
f unis.
F7sus
C2/G
C2/E
f
50
unis.
come help us see,
shine in Your full - ness, let Your
Opt. Tenors only
C2/F
G7sus
G
C2
C2/E

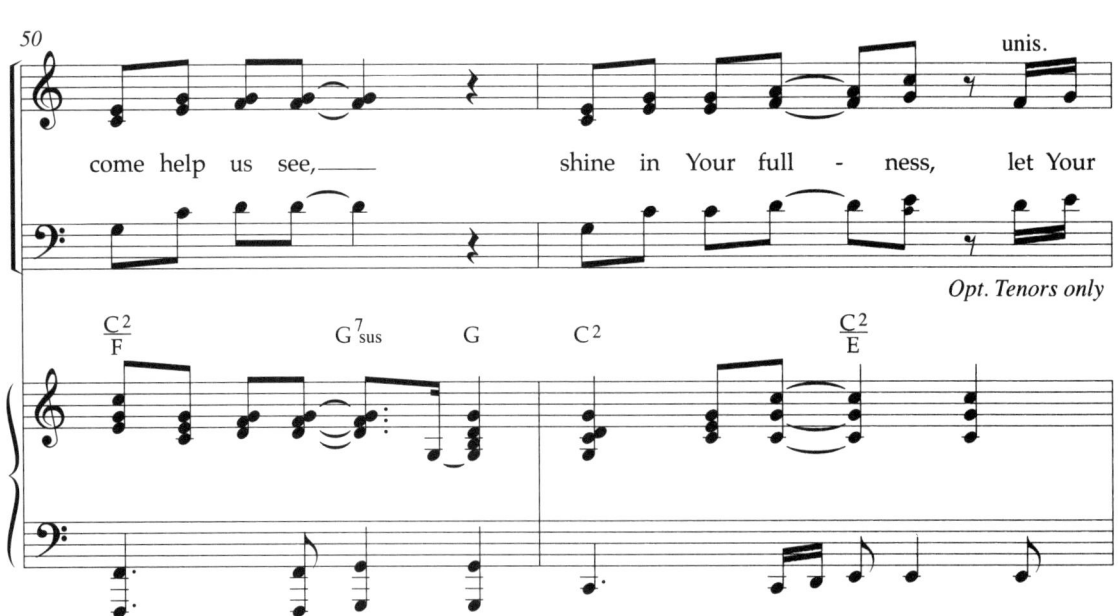

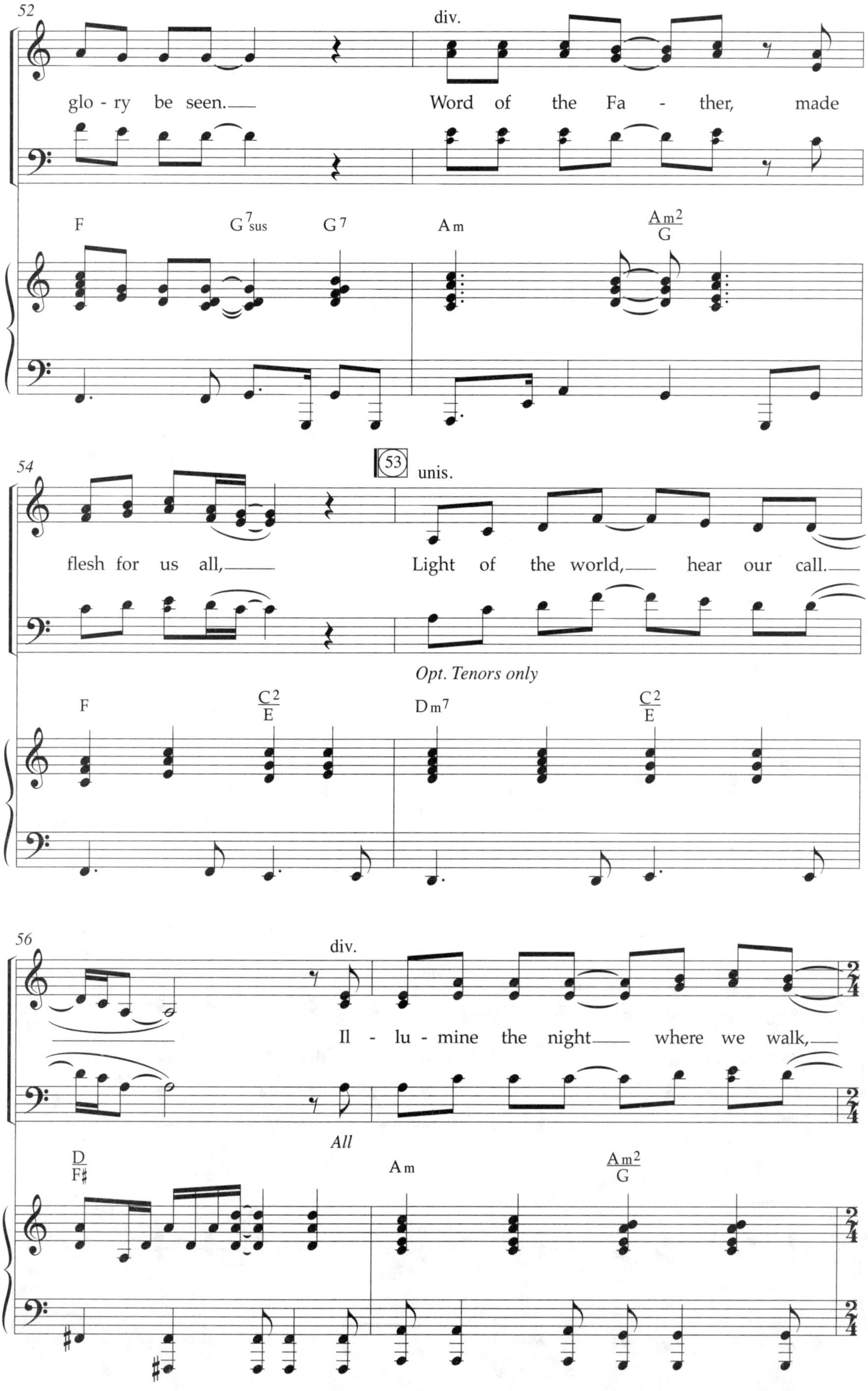
52
div.
glo - ry be seen.
Word of the Fa - ther, made
F G7sus G7 Am Am2/G
54
53
unis.
flesh for us all,
Light of the world, hear our call.
Opt. Tenors only
F C2/E Dm7 C2/E
56
div.
Il - lu - mine the night where we walk,
All
D/F♯ Am Am2/G
2/4

Come light— Your world.

Come light— Your world.

Thou Didst Leave Thy Throne

EMILY E. S. ELLIOTT

TIMOTHY R. MATTHEWS
Arranged by Kim Noblitt

10

Beth - le - hem's home was there found no room for Thy ho - ly na - tiv - i -

C   B7   Em   Cm6/Eb   G/D   Am7/D

13

unis.   div.

- ty.   O   come to my heart, Lord   Je - sus,   There is

unis.   div.

Dm7/G   G9   C/E   F M7   G/F

16   55   unis.

room in my heart for   Thee.

unis.

MEN unis.

mf Heav - en's

Em7 Am7   Dm9 G7   C   C2⁴   C   C2⁴/Bb   C/Bb   C2/Bb

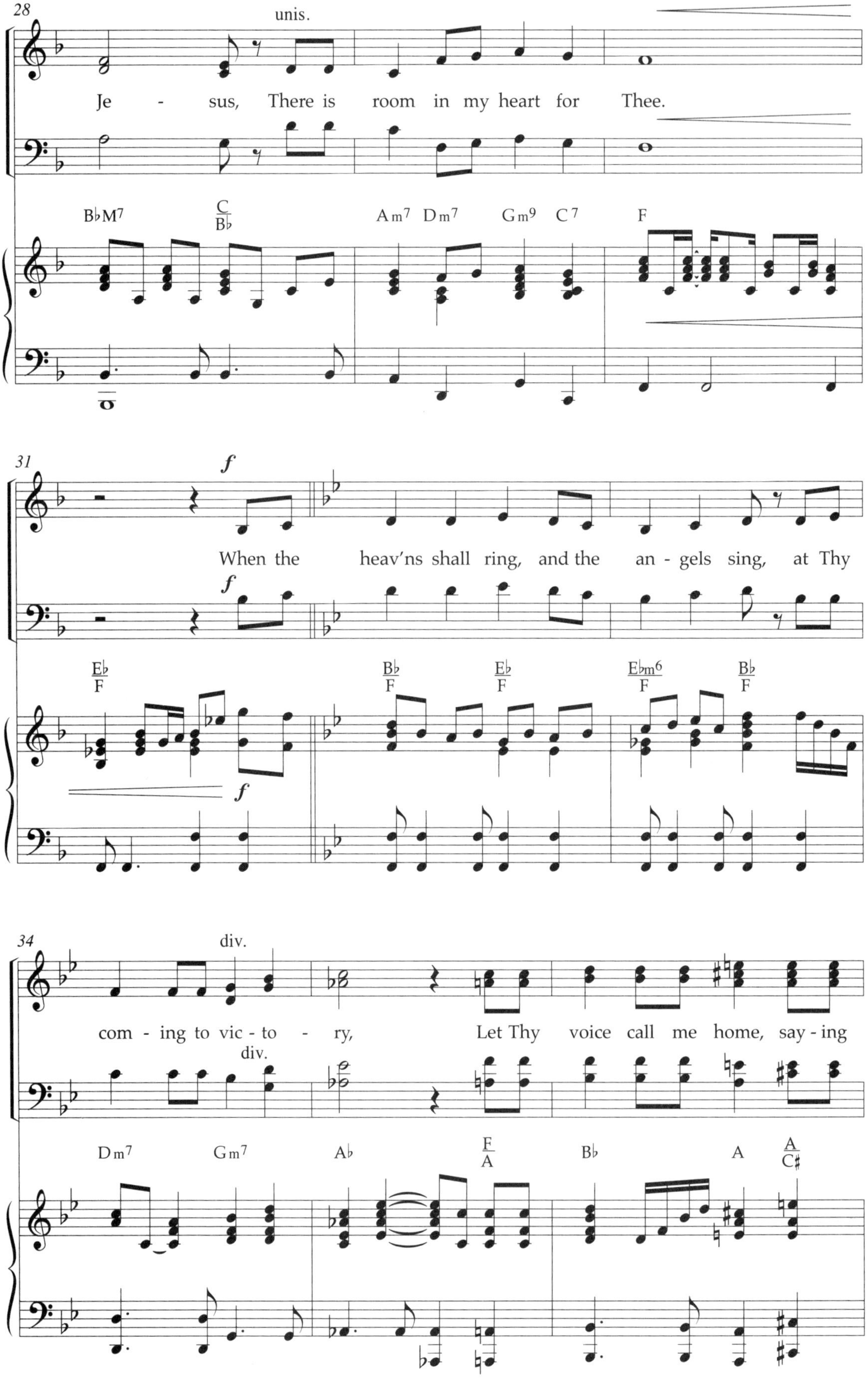
28
unis.
Je - sus, There is room in my heart for Thee.
B♭M7
C/B♭
Am7 Dm7 Gm9 C7
F
31
f
When the heav'ns shall ring, and the an - gels sing, at Thy
E♭/F
B♭/F
E♭/F
E♭m6/F
B♭/F
34
div.
com - ing to vic - to - ry, Let Thy voice call me home, say - ing
Dm7 Gm7 A♭ F/A B♭ A A/C♯

room   in   my   heart   for   Thee.

Willing
Narration

Music by KIM NOBLITT
Arranged by J. Daniel Smith

*NARRATOR 2: Lord God, we know that You did not have to come.

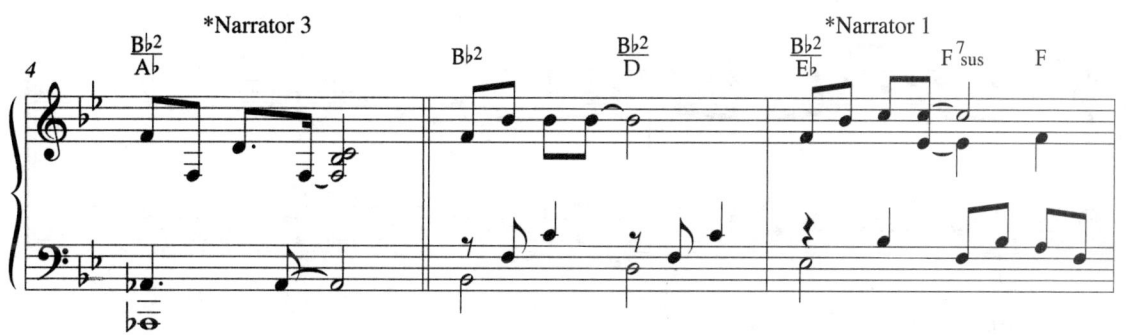

*NARRATOR 3: Lord God, we know that Your redemptive plan didn't have to include us—we don't know how, we don't know why.

*NARRATOR 1: But we do know this: we know we love You.

*NARRATOR 2: We know that we are here today only by Your mercy.

*NARRATOR 3: We know that the only place we want to be tonight is right here, right now, together at Your feet,

*NARRATOR 1: crowning You as King,

*NARRATOR 2: exalting You as Lord,

*NARRATOR 3: praising You, Lamb of God,

*NARRATOR 2: for being worthy, and being willing to come to us,

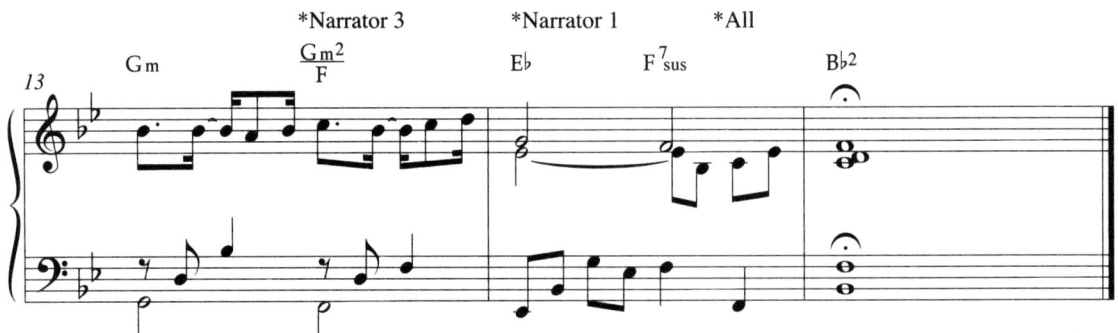

*NARRATOR 3: to rescue us,

*NARRATOR 1: and to make us a part of Your kingdom—

*ALL: Your kingdom that will never, never end.

We Crown You Lord of All

with
O Holy Night
O Come, All Ye Faithful
Solo and Choir

Words and Music by
MIKE HARLAND and KIM NOBLITT
Arranged by J. Daniel Smith

You are God's glo - ry, His on-ly—

— Son,　　the Bright-est Morn - ing,　　the Ho - ly One.

† "O Holy Night." Words and Music Adolphe Adam, Chappeau de Roquemaure, and John S. Dwight.

104

CHOIR *(Soloist may continue)*

18
mf

Glo - ry to the Son of God, who was and is and now has

mf

C/G   G   C/E   D/F♯   G   C   G/B

mf

21
unis.

come. Glo - ry to the King who knows no end, we

unis.

D sus   D   C/G   G   C/E   D/F♯   Em

24
1 ⑥¹

crown You Lord of all. We crown You Lord of all.

C   D   Em   Em²/D   1 C   D

† "O Come, All Ye Faithful." Words Latin Hymn, ascribed to John Francis Wade. Music John Francis Wade.

His Kingdom Shall Never End

with
Hallelujah Chorus

Words and Music by KIM NOBLITT
Arranged by J. Daniel Smith

*NARRATOR 3: Yes, we crown Him Lord of all—the One who has come down from heaven and poured out Christmas blessing on the undeserving. We crown only one King—Jesus Christ—the King whose kingdom will never end!

112

114

† "Hallelujah Chorus." Words and Music George Frederick Handel.

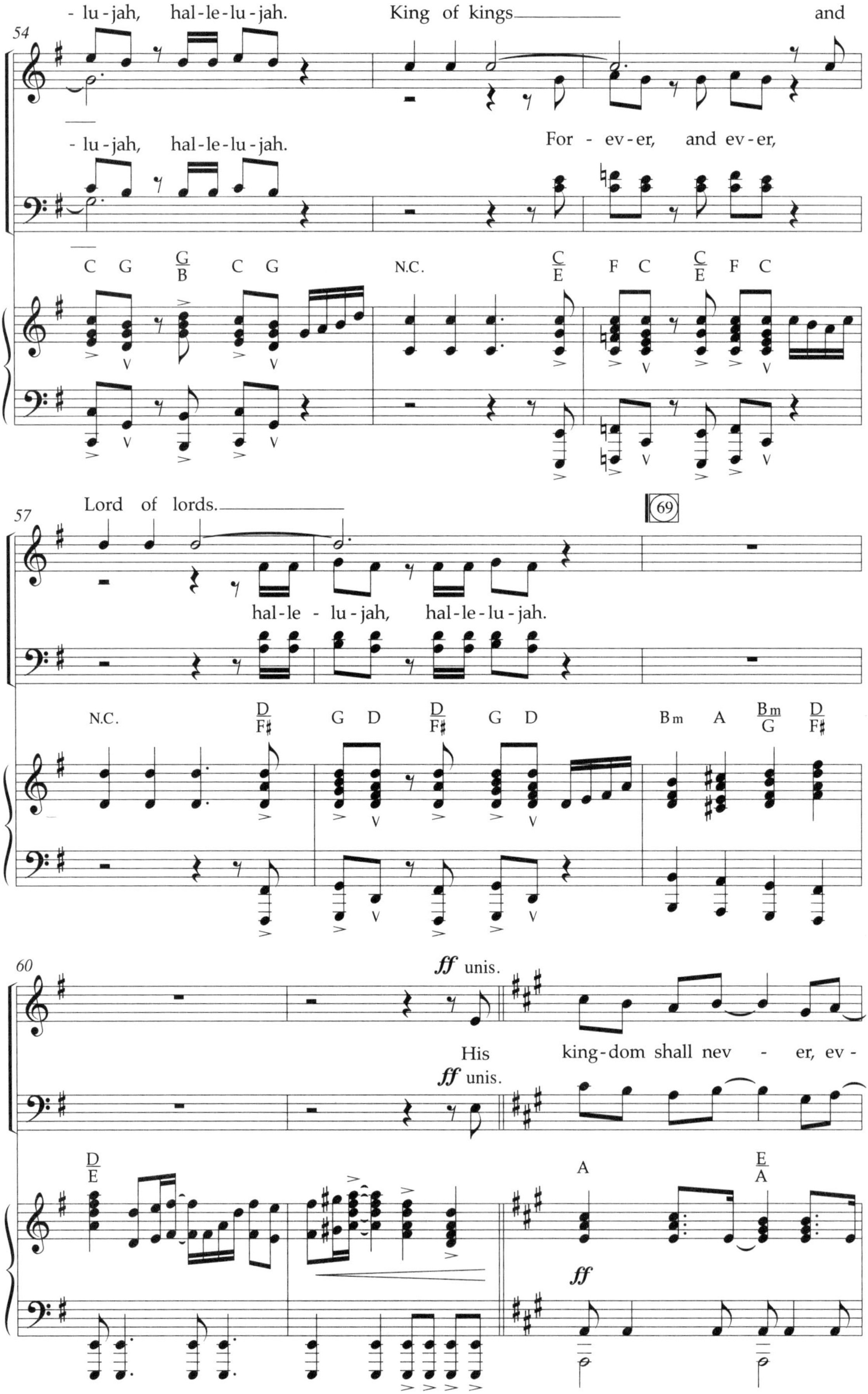
-lu-jah, hal-le-lu-jah. King of kings and
54
-lu-jah, hal-le-lu-jah. For-ev-er, and ev-er,
C G G/B C G N.C. C/E F C C/E F C
Lord of lords.
57
69
hal-le-lu-jah, hal-le-lu-jah.
N.C. D/F♯ G D D/F♯ G D Bm A Bm/G D/F♯
60
ff unis.
His king-dom shall nev - er, ev-
ff unis.
D/E A E/A
ff